See Like Me

Diana Noonan

A bee

An owl

Can they see like me?

A dog

A fly

I see a flower.

A bee sees the flower.

I see a mouse.

An owl sees the mouse.

I see a cake.

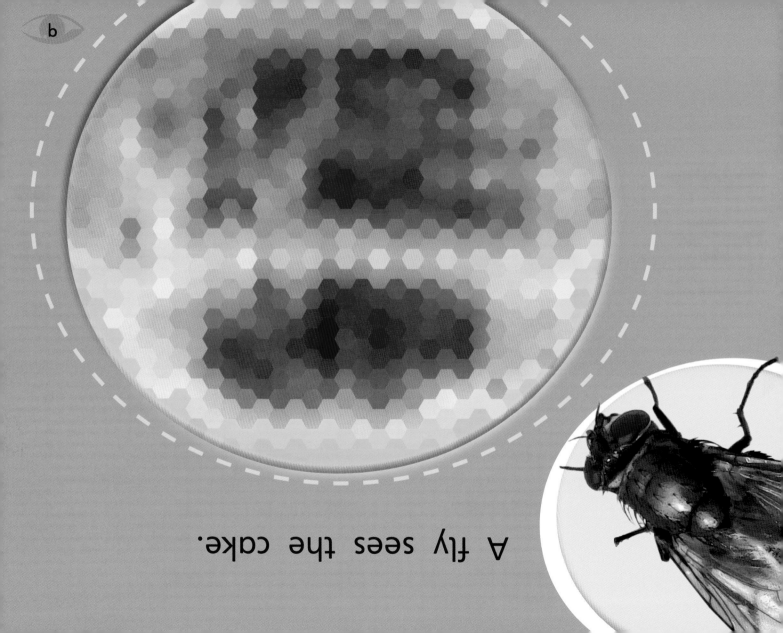

A fly sees the cake.

I see my dad.

My dog sees my dad.

I see

A bee sees

I see

An owl sees

I see

A fly sees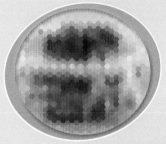

I see

A dog sees